The Power of Silence

Finding Peace, Purpose, and Connection in a Noisy World

KISHORE MUTALIKDESAI

DEDICATION

This book is dedicated to my dear readers.

CONTENTS

INTRODUCTION

Have you ever noticed the power of silence? How can it transform the world's chaos into a peaceful sanctuary? In what way does it provide clarity for a cluttered mind? How it can forge deeper connections with others? These questions have consumed my thoughts for years, and they are the queries that led me on a journey to discover the profound impact of silence on our lives.

I invite you to join me on this journey as we explore the incredible power of silence in my book, "The Power of Silence: Finding Peace, Purpose, and Connection in a Noisy World." In these pages, I will take you on a philosophical, spiritual, and scientific exploration of silence, uncovering its secrets and revealing its transformative effects on our relationships, our personal growth, and our overall well-being.

Picture yourself in a bustling city, surrounded by the honking horns, the chatter of strangers, and the never-ending cacophony of life. It is overwhelming, isn't it? We live in a world that constantly bombards us with noise and distractions, pulling us away from what matters. Amidst this chaos, there lies a hidden power, a power that can harness to find peace, purpose, and connection.

Silence is the antidote to the noise. It is the relief we search for, the shelter where we can withdraw and discover tranquillity. External clamour often drowns our inner voices out, but in the silence, we can listen to ourselves. It is in the silence that we can cultivate self-awareness, nourish our minds, and rediscover our true purpose. It is in the silence that we can create space for personal growth and transformation.

Silence is not just an individual pursuit. It has the power to impact our relationships, both in the corporate world and within our families. In the corporate world, people often undervalue silence and dismiss it as a sign of weakness or indifference. What if I told you that embracing silence can lead to stronger relationships, increased productivity, and enhanced problem-solving skills? By fostering an environment where we respect and encourage silence, we can create a space for open communication, innovative thinking, and a deeper understanding of one another.

Within our families, silence can transform the way we connect with our loved ones. In a world filled with constant distractions, finding moments of silence together can strengthen the bonds that hold us together. In silence, we find the space to listen, comprehend, and meet each other's needs and desires. The silence allows us to listen to one another, understand each other's needs and desires. It is during moments of quietude that we can forge deep connections that can withstand any challenge.

Throughout this book, I will share narratives of ordinary people who have embraced the power of silence and transformed their lives in extraordinary ways. From corporate leaders who have revolutionized their businesses through the practice of silence, to families who have found renewed love and understanding through shared moments of quiet reflection, their stories will inspire and motivate you to do the same.

I invite you to tune out the noise, to embrace the silence, and to embark on a journey towards finding peace, purpose, and connection in a noisy world. Together, we will explore the depths of silence, unlocking its secrets and harnessing its power to transform our lives. I hope this book will not merely educate, entertain, and inspire you to seek the beauty and strength that lies within the power of silence. Together, let us start this journey and uncover the magical surprises that await   us.

CHAPTER 1

Unveiling the Path to Peace, Purpose, and Connection in a Noisy World

The Power of Silence

As I sit down to write this chapter, I cannot help but experience a soothing calm wash over me. The subject of silence has always captivated me, resonating in my core. In this loud, chaotic world of ours, where information bombards us from every direction, the power of silence often goes unnoticed. But, my friend, if we could only tap into its transformative abilities, we could find the peace, purpose, and connection we yearn for.

Silence holds a deeper meaning beyond just the lack of sound. It delves much deeper than that. It is a state of mind, a sanctuary that offers us individual protection when the chaos threatens to overwhelm us. Amid our modern lives, filled with constant demands and never-ending distractions, discovering moments of stillness can be quite challenging. Yet, if we create space for silence, we can unlock its profound benefits.

One of the most beautiful gifts that silence gives people is the clarity. By detaching ourselves from external distractions, we create space for our inner voice to surface. It is in the silence where our thoughts transition into crystal clear understanding, where our emotions solidify, and where our genuine desires emerge from the depths of our soul.

I remember a moment during a silent meditation retreat that remains etched in my mind, vivid and electrifying. It had been days since I had uttered a single word, and as my mind settled into the stillness, clarity washed over me like a gentle wave caressing the shore. My life's path became crystal clear in that magical moment. It swept away the noise and confusion that had clouded my mind, leaving behind a sense of purpose that filled me with renewed energy.

Focus is yet another incredible outcome of embracing silence. In our fast-paced world, our attention is being pulled in a thousand different directions- with notifications, messages, and demands that tear our focus to shreds, leaving us with a sense of being overwhelmed. But, my friend, when we choose to create moments of quiet in our lives, we give ourselves a chance to regain our attention.

During my years in the IT industry, I drowned in an ocean of emails, deadlines, and never-ending meetings. Escape seemed impossible, like chasing windmills. But amidst that chaos, I discovered the power of the brief breaks of silence. During those precious moments, I could reset my mind and regain my focus. Ignoring the world around me, I zeroed in on the task. The result? Witnessing a remarkable surge in productivity and the capacity to tackle challenging problems with ease.

Now, the most valuable gift of all, my friend, lies deep within the silence — inner peace. In this dizzying, turbulent world we inhabit, inner peace can often seem distant, an intangible dream hovering just beyond our reach. But hear me now. The moment we surrender to silence, we open the doorways of our soul to journey inward, to connect with the stillness nestled at our core.

In a time of turmoil, I found solace in silent meditation. Chaos reigned in the external world, but within the silence, I found solace. As I take a breath, my inner self released the accumulated tension and turmoil. In that sacred space of silence, a profound sense of peace has embraced me, transcending the external circumstances. From that peaceful realm, I approached my challenges with unwavering resilience and a grounded presence.

The transformative power of silence does not live within us as individuals. It has the strength to create profound shifts in our relationships and communities, too. In a world where we often experience solitude, silence becomes the bridge that connects us. By embracing silence together, we create spaces for deep listening and genuine understanding.

I witnessed this power firsthand during a workshop on mindful communication. Through their active involvement in guided silence, the participants created a noticeable shift in the room's energy. Walls that had once stood tall between them crumbled away, and a sense of unity bloomed. In that silence, it rendered words meaningless. The quiet presence of everyone spoke volumes, forming a language of its own. This powerful reminder showed that sometimes we forge the most profound connections without words.

How can you harness the transformative power of silence in your own life? It starts with setting aside intentional time for it. This might mean incorporating meditation into your daily routine or finding moments throughout the day to disconnect from the noise and immerse yourself in stillness. It requires cultivating an awareness of the present moment and choosing to prioritize silence in a world that often glorifies noise.

In my journey of unravelling the power of silence, I realize it is not a destination, but an ongoing practice. It is a dance between embracing the silence and learning to listen to the whispers of our hearts. It is an everlasting invitation to slow down, tune in, and allow the wisdom of silence to guide us towards a life of profound peace, clarity, and connection.

In the pages that follow, my dear friend, I will share stories of ordinary people who have embraced silence and experienced its life-changing effects. Through their experiences, we will embark on a deep exploration of the power of silence and how we can wield it to shape our existence, brimming with clarity, focus, and inner peace.

Will you join me now on this life-changing journey as we traverse the paths that lead to the heart of silence? Together, let us explore the strength it possesses to illuminate our lives, awakening the very core of who we are.

The Benefits of Silence

In the crazy, fast-paced world we live in, finding silence is like stumbling upon a hidden treasure. Trust me, I get it. We cannot escape noise no matter where we go - cars honk, people chatter, TVs blare, and our phones buzz without end. The incessant noise never allows us a moment of peace. But here is the thing: silence has this incredible power that can bring us back to ourselves, give us peace, and help us find our purpose and connection.

Silence speaks. Though mute, it conveys meaning. In the unspoken, we find deeper truths - insight unclouded by noise. Silence calms our turbulent minds, enriching the space between sounds. Its voiceless message echoes wisdom within. It is so much more than that. This incredible superpower can restore our sense of wholeness in a chaotic world. When we welcome silence into our lives, we open to a whole range of benefits that have the potential to transform our well-being in ways we never imagined.

Quietness can erase stress, which is one of its greatest advantages. Stress is like that clingy friend that just will not leave us alone. Work, relationships, and life can become overwhelming. When we take some time to soak in the silence, we give ourselves permission to catch our breath and recharge. The stillness that comes with silence lets our minds rest and our bodies relax, releasing the tension that stress clings to. Science says that even a few minutes of silence a day can lower our cortisol levels, this hormone that likes to stir up stress. So, by weaving moments of silence into our daily routines, we can find this calm, balanced state that helps us tackle life's curveballs with a little more grace.

Wait, there is more! Silence is not good for our stress levels; it has got some serious benefits for our mental health too. In a world where everything is screaming for our attention, our thoughts are running at lightning speed. Our thoughts race like an unstoppable train, jumping from one idea to another without pause. All this inner chatter has the tendency to be downright exhausting, leading to anxiety, depression, and a whole slew of other issues. But when we embrace silence, we are giving our minds the space to breathe and rejuvenate. It is like we are ignoring the external noise and turning inward. During that silence, we can release worries and distractions that overwhelm our minds. Studies have even shown that meditation, which often involves silence, can do wonders for our emotional well-being, reducing symptoms of anxiety and depression. Silence is not just a momentary escape; it can ignite a total transformation, making us more in tune with ourselves and helping us develop the resilience we need to face life's hurdles.

Guess what? The beauty of silence does not stop at just helping ourselves; it is a game-changer for our relationships too. In a world where everyone seems to compete for attention, silence becomes this secret weapon for genuine listening. When we quiet our thoughts and judgments, we create space for others to speak and to be heard. We immerse ourselves in their words, soaking up their perspective and emotions with no distractions. When we gift someone the tranquillity of silence, we show them that their words and experiences matter to us. Silence becomes this bridge that connects us on a whole other level, allowing for authentic and deep connections that enrich our relationships. Instead of communication just being about words, it becomes this powerful exchange of emotions and understanding. Silence opens the door to empathy and compassion, empowering us to build stronger bonds with the people in our lives.

When contemplating the power of silence, one story comes to mind. It is the story of Sarah, this young professional whose life was on the verge of becoming a chaotic tornado. Sarah was racing against the clock, trying to meet deadlines and meet everyone's expectations. She desired a moment of tranquillity, an opportunity to reconnect with herself and tune into her own thoughts. So, one day, she decided it was time for a change. She started waking up a few minutes earlier each day, using the silence of the early morning hours to find solace and clarity. She allowed herself to sit in silence, with no distractions, and just be. And guess what? It made all the difference. She noticed her stress levels decrease, and she felt an overall improvement in her well-being. Sarah's journey with silence inspired others around her to seek peace.

However, my friend, silence does not limit itself to a select few. It is available to every single one of us if we are open to embracing it. In moments of silence, we find strength, clarity, and peace to face challenges, decide, and connect with others. Do not forget the power of silence as we navigate this noisy world. Let us carve out those moments of peace amidst the chaos and allow ourselves to find purpose, connection, and that much-needed peace we all crave.

Embracing Silence

In my journey of self-discovery, I have stumbled upon this mind-blowing concept: silence. It has got some extraordinary power. Close your eyes and imagine a serene scene where silence reigns and your thoughts are the only sound. Pure stillness allows us to connect with ourselves and the world. It is like a secret rendezvous with our own minds, where we get to reflect on its wonders.

Now, before you picture me as some kind of silent hermit, let me clarify. Embracing silence does not mean shutting ourselves off from the world like a fortress. No, no. It is important to carve out time for reflection and introspection in our lives. Need a break amidst all the noise.

Before we explore embracing silence, let us take a moment to appreciate its beauty. During the quietness, we gain clarity, insight, and the ability to listen to our inner voice. In that quiet space, we can become super aware and tap into our true selves.

Now that we understand the point, let us talk. How can we incorporate silence into our everyday hustle and bustle? Get ready to embrace silence like a pro with these tips and tricks I have up my sleeve.

Start by creating intentional silence for yourself. In a noisy and distracting world, intentional silence is a rare gem. Reserve daily moments of silence. Whether it is morning or night, it could be five minutes or an hour before bedtime. Find what works for you and stick to it. Use that time to meditate, journal, or just sit still and let your thoughts roam free.

Next up, create yourself a sacred space. Seek a peaceful location indoors or outdoors for moments of quiet reflection. This space should be your personal sanctuary, stuffed to the brim with peace and tranquillity. Decorate it with things that bring you joy and help calm your soul. It is your refuge from the chaos of the world, so make it count.

It is time to embrace mindfulness. Mindfulness means being present, without judgment or attachments. By practicing mindfulness, we can become more aware of our thoughts, emotions, and surroundings. So, try incorporating it into your daily routine. Focus on your breath, pay attention to your thoughts and sensations, and do whatever you do with full-on presence. Experience joy through walking, eating, or embracing the sounds of the world. Through the act of linking with our inner selves during periods of silence, we come across the serenity and contentment we have yearned for. Establishing a deep connection with our inner selves during moments of silence brings the peace and fulfilment we have been longing for. In the process of seeking peace and fulfilment, we form a bond with our inner selves through moments of silence. It is all part of embracing the sweet sound of silence.

While we are at it, let us talk about distractions. Our lives are crawling with them, always trying to pry us away from our only quiet friend. So do yourself a favour and limit those distractions. Maybe turn off those pesky notifications on your phone, carve out device-free zones in your home, or let others know you need some alone time. The world will wait for you, but what about your inner truth? In moments of silence, we discover inner peace and fulfilment. and a portal to mindfulness. Yes, that is hiding in the silence.

In spending time alone, let us not overlook solitude. Although it may seem like a scary abyss of loneliness, it is, in fact, a gift. Solitude provides the chance to be alone with our thoughts and emotions, and one experiences an empowering calm. So, embrace it! Do things that bring you joy, that let you reflect on life. Take a nature walk, immerse yourself in a book, or sit in silence. Solitude can change you, my friend.

How about using silence for deep self-reflection? It is like a date with your own soul, where you get to ask yourself some real deep questions. What makes you happy? What do you believe in? What are the challenges you are facing? Grab a journal and write your thoughts and insights. Trust me, it is in those quiet moments that our inner truths unravel.

Embracing silence is not a onetime event. It is a practice, a commitment to ourselves. There are moments when our minds resist stillness, perceiving the outside world as loud. But stick with it, my friend.

The more you embrace silence, the more natural it will become in your daily life.

In this fast-paced world, we underestimate the power of silence. If we incorporate it into our routines and activities, we will find peace, purpose, and a connection unlike anything we have experienced before. So let silence become your tool for self-discovery and transformation. Watch the world grow quiet and your inner voice grows louder. Trust me, you will not regret it.

Silence and Mindfulness

So here I am, diving headfirst into the mysterious abyss that is the connection between silence and mindfulness. It is like a rollercoaster ride of self-discovery, a wild adventure through the depths of my mind.

I picture this: I am sitting cross-legged in a cozy nook, surrounded by a symphony of silence. The air is thick with anticipation, as if holding its breath, waiting for me to unravel the secrets hidden within the stillness. I sense my heart thumping in my chest with a mix of anticipation and apprehension, pondering what I will experience on this adventure.

As I close my eyes, the world around me disappears, and I voyage through the vast landscape of my thoughts. It is a whirlwind of emotions, memories, and imaginings - like a wild river rushing through the canyons of my mind. The current carries me along and sometimes with the turbulent force of a storm, but always leading me closer to the truth.

Amidst the chaos, moments of stillness and tranquillity emerge, allowing me to be present. Pause and reflect on this remarkable research. It is in these moments that I find myself mindful, aware of my thoughts, my emotions, and the world around me.

Silence is captivating, embodying both the quietness and a doorway to mindful awareness. Silence offers an opportunity to connect with our inner selves and find the peace and fulfilment we have been seeking. The contrast between the frenzied flurry of thoughts and the serene calm of silence amplifies the power of each experience. It is like a dance between chaos and serenity, a beautiful symphony of contrast.

And with each step I take along this path, the suspense grows. What will I discover next? What truths will I discover? It is both exhilarating and intimidating, this exploration of the connection between silence and mindfulness.

The more I explore, the more I understand how universally relatable this journey is. We all have our own silences to explore, our own minds to navigate. We all yearn for moments of stillness in a world that never stops spinning. In this shared quest for self-discovery, we find a sense of connection, a shared understanding of what it means to be human.

So, as I continue this path, I invite you to join me - to embrace the contrasts, to experience the suspense, and to immerse yourselves in the vivid imagery that silence and mindfulness can bring. Together, let us venture into the unknown and unravel the secrets that lie within the depths of our own minds.

The Science of Silence

I started diving into the scientific research studies on the mind-blowing power of silence. I could not believe my eyes. Several studies have delved into the effects of silence on our brains, bodies, and well-being. With each dive, I become more aware of how this journey resonates with everyone. The results were mind-blowing. Silence can do wonders for us.

Researchers from Stanford University conducted an epic study to examine the brain's response to prolonged silence. Turns out, silence can make our brains grow new cells in this cool region called the hippocampus - that is the part responsible for learning and memory. Brief moments of peace can enhance IQ.

Now, get this: there was another study, published in the journal, 'Heart' that investigated how silence affects our blood pressure and heart rate. Those who experienced silence came up with cooler ideas and solutions. Discovering moments of tranquillity now and then could enhance our IQ. They investigated how silence affects our blood pressure and heart rate. They found just two minutes of silence can lower our blood pressure and slow down our heart rate. It is like putting the brakes on stress and giving our hearts a well-deserved break. Pretty good, right?

That is not all. Silence has some serious mind-boosting capabilities too. Researchers from the University of California, Berkeley, discovered that silence can be the ultimate stress-buster. When we soak up some silence, this part of our brain called the default mode network kicks into high gear. It is like a superpower that brings calm and tranquillity to our minds, leaving stress and anxiety in the dust.

Wait, there is more! Scientists at the University of Illinois conducted an epic study that showed how silence can enhance our creativity and problem-solving skills. Half of the people working on something creative faced noise, while the other half enjoyed peace. Those who enjoyed silence generated cooler ideas and solutions. When you struggle to merge your thoughts, find a quiet spot, and let your mind work its magic.

Silence is not something vague. It is legit therapeutic, especially in mindfulness and meditation. Many of the studies have shown that making silence a regular part of our lives can improve our mental well-being. It is like a natural antidepressant or anxiety antidote. People who spend time in silence, whether it is through meditation or just taking some quiet moments, have reported experiencing increased happiness, peace, and reduced stress. That is some serious inner peace mojo right there!

One study at Harvard Medical School even showed that silence can change our brain structure. Yes, you heard me right. Regular moments of silence can give our attention and sensory processing skills a nice little makeover. So, not only will silence help us focus better, but it will also give us better control over our emotions. Talk about a win-win!

Pause and contemplate this incredible research. Silence extends beyond seeking tranquillity in our chaotic world. It opens the door to something deeper. It is a magical key that unlocks self-understanding and knowledge of the world. Silence allows us to connect with our inner selves, finding the peace and fulfilment we desire.

Let us explore some inspiring stories. People, like us, embracing the life-changing impact of silence. Entrepreneurs who swear that moments of quiet reflection have sparked their most brilliant business ideas. Athletes who use the power of silence to visualize their way to success. These awesome individuals have discovered that silence is the secret ingredient to unlocking their full potential and reaching greatness.

Here is the deal. I will not leave you hanging with these mind-blowing research and stories. I am going to take you on a wild ride through the science of silence and share some jaw-dropping real-life examples of its profound impact. Together, we are going to learn how to harness the power of silence in our own lives and find the peace, purpose, and connection we crave.

So, let us strap in and embark on this epic journey of discovery. Let us embrace the power of silence and unleash the mind-blowing potential that lies within.

Amid this crazy chaos, silence will be our guiding light, our oasis of clarity, and our compass towards a life that is meaningful and fulfilling.

CHAPTER 2

Silence in Corporate Relationships

Silent Listening

Have you ever noticed the magic that happens when someone listens to you without interrupting or imposing themselves? It is like they create this sacred space where they listen to and comprehend your words. I have seen this transformative power of silent listening firsthand throughout my career in various industries. Those who master this skill excel and build genuine connections from the boardroom to the shop floor.

Silent listening is more than just hearing words. It is about immersing yourself in a conversation, capturing the emotions and perspectives being conveyed with no agenda or judgment. It is about creating an openness and receptivity that allows the speaker to express themselves.

But let us not forget about active listening. It is the art of responding to someone that shows them you get what they are saying. It involves paraphrasing, asking questions to clarify, and giving feedback that shows genuine understanding. Active listening is like the perfect partner for silent listening; together, they create a force for transformation and connection.

The power of silence lies in its ability to give us a moment of reflection and introspection. Pausing in conversation allows us to process and make meaning from what we share. By embracing these silent moments, we go beyond the surface level and tap into the essence of what someone is trying to communicate.

Silent listening also allows us to pick up on nonverbal cues that speak volumes. Facial expressions, body language, and tone of voice all contribute to the deeper meanings and emotions being conveyed. When we pay attention to these silent signals, we gain a fuller understanding of someone's intentions, struggles, and triumphs. We can empathize with them and appreciate their unique perspective.

In the workplace, we cannot emphasize the importance of silent listening enough. Whether it is team meetings, one-on-one interactions, or presentations, listening and embracing moments of silence can create a culture of trust, inclusivity, and innovation. When everyone senses that they are listened to and respected, collaboration and problem-solving reach new heights.

I will never forget the time I witnessed the power of silent listening in action during a project kick-off meeting. The room was buzzing with excitement, but one team member, Maya, remained silent. Her calm demeanour and attentive presence drew everyone's attention. As the meeting progressed, Maya listened, absorbing every idea and suggestion. And when it was her turn to speak, her words were like pearls of wisdom. Her silence had allowed her to understand the discussion and respond with clarity and insight. She became a trusted leader in the team, all because of her choice to embrace silent listening.

Silent listening is not a passive act. It is a deliberate and active decision. Building a connection with others requires discipline, patience, and a genuine desire. Instead of trying to make sure our voices are heard, we are encouraged to understand and appreciate others' perspectives. We can hone and cultivate the skill over time, and it offers immense rewards.

In conclusion, active listening and the power of silence are game-changers in understanding and connecting with colleagues and superiors. When we embrace silent listening, we create a space for empathy, understanding, and connection. We create an environment where we appreciate diverse perspectives and foster collaboration and innovation. So, as we navigate this noisy world, let us remember the transformative power of silence and unleash its potential in every interaction and relationship.

Silence in Conflict Resolution

Silence possesses a mysterious power that can resolve conflicts and impact on various aspects of life. I mean, think about it: silence can create a safe space for people to have honest conversations and find peaceful resolutions. In this chapter, we delve into how silence can improve our relationships.

To start, let us define "conflict" before discussing the power of silence in resolving it. If we do not handle conflicts, they can escalate quick and turn any relationship into a war zone. Conflict resolution involves finding a solution that satisfies everyone involved. It is about finding a solution that benefits everyone and promoting better cooperation and understanding.

Now, one key ingredient in conflict resolution is creating a safe space for open and honest dialogue. And guess what? The secret ingredient for making that happen is silence. When we embrace silence, it gives us the chance to listen — I mean listen — without interrupting or judging. Self-expression is like opening a door, enabling people to have their thoughts acknowledged and comprehended. So, here are some strategies for using silence in conflict resolution.

First up, we have got active listening. Active listening involves giving undivided attention to the speaker without interruptions. And silence plays a big part in helping us do that. When we lend our ears, it enables the other person to experience being listened to and understood, which is a fundamental shift in resolving conflicts.

Next, let us talk about pausing and reflecting. You know how sometimes conflicts just blow up because we react without thinking? By pausing and taking a moment of silence before responding, we can prevent that. It gives us the chance to gather our thoughts, process the information, and respond in a more composed and constructive way. Plus, it shows respect for the other person's perspective—we are taking the time to consider it before offering our own.

Silence encompasses more than just our words—it includes our non-verbal communication as well. Can silence be a powerful non-verbal tool in conflict resolution? You know, things like softening our facial expressions, maintaining eye contact, and nodding in agreement—all of that can create a safe space for the other person to share their thoughts and emotions. By embracing silence in our non-verbal communication, we are showing our willingness to listen to their thoughts, and we hold their perspective in high regard.

And sometimes conflicts require some serious introspection. Allowing room for reflection is important in that context. We all need our space, right? Well, silence can provide the space for reflection. It lets us gather our thoughts and gain a deeper understanding of our own emotions and motivations. When we encourage moments of silence in discussions, we are giving ourselves the freedom to explore our own feelings and consider the impact of our actions. That kind of self-reflection is key to resolving conflicts.

Group settings can also be a breeding ground for conflicts, not just one-on-one situations. That can be a challenge. But by embracing silence, we can contribute to a more peaceful resolution. Encouraging moments of silence in group discussions nurtures an environment for individuals to reflect on their thoughts before expressing them. It also discourages interruptions and gives each person an equal chance to contribute. And that fosters a sense of equality and respect within the group.

Now, let us talk about mindfulness. Yes, it has become a buzzword these days, but it is useful in conflict resolution. Mindfulness means being present and aware of your thoughts and actions. By incorporating mindfulness techniques into conflict resolution, you can cultivate a sense of calm and clarity. Stepping back aids in gaining objectivity during the moment. It lets you identify your own triggers and reactions, leading to more thoughtful and compassionate solutions.

And, when conflicts seem impossible to crack, do not be afraid to seek mediation. That is when you bring in a neutral third party to help facilitate communication between the conflicting parties. And guess what? Silence can be a handy tool during those mediation sessions. It gives everyone a chance to gather their thoughts and share them without interruptions. Mediators can use silence to create a safe space for dialogue, encouraging people to listen to each other's perspectives and work toward finding a resolution.

So, there you have it—silence can be a super powerful tool for conflict resolution. By listening, pausing, and reflecting, using non-verbal communication, allowing room for reflection, embracing silence in group settings, applying mindfulness techniques, and seeking mediation, you can create a safe space for open and honest dialogue. When you resolve conflicts, it leads to stronger relationships and a deeper understanding of each other.

Silence and Leadership

As I dove deeper into the world of silence, something fascinating hit me like a ton of bricks - the incredible connection between silence and leadership. It is remarkable how silence can guide others in unexpected ways. Intrigued by this newfound revelation, I set out on a mission to uncover how leaders could harness the power of silence to inspire their teams, ignite their creativity, and make those oh-so-important decisions.

People often overlook the power of silence in a world that never stops talking. But once I dug beneath the surface, I realized that silence has this incredible ability to create a calm and focused environment - and that is a significant change for any leader worth their salt. When a leader embraces silence, they are giving their team the space to reflect and dig deep within themselves to find their own voice, their own ideas, and their own solutions.

To further explore this mind-boggling concept, I started digging into the experiences of leaders who have mastered the art of silence in their leadership styles. One of these incredible leaders was Emily Chen, the CEO of a tech startup. She tells us all about how she incorporates moments of silence during team meetings, encouraging her team to take a breather and think about the problem at hand. And guess what? Those moments of silence worked their magic! Emily noticed her team becoming more engaged, more creative, and they generated innovative solutions they would have never thought of amid all the noise and chaos.

It turns out that silence not only unlocks creativity but also supercharges decision-making. The Harvard Business School study explained that teams who took a moment of silence before making important decisions exhibited higher levels of critical thinking and reached well-reasoned conclusions. This makes sense when you think about it - silence gives individuals the space to process information without all those annoying external distractions screaming for attention.

But wait, there is more! Silence can also be a powerful tool for connection. When leaders embrace silence, they are creating a space for others to open up and share their thoughts and experiences. Richard Turner, an absolute pro in the business world, who spilled all the beans for us. He is a firm advocate for incorporating silence in one-on-one meetings. He seeks an answer through a question. Through this simple act, Richard builds trust, strengthens connections, and creates a team that is engaged to the maximum. The result? Productivity through the roof.

Silence does not imply disengagement or communication shutdown. The best leaders know how to strike that perfect balance between silence, active listening, and clear communication. They understand that silence can facilitate real, meaningful conversations, but it must go hand in hand with a genuine desire to understand others. These leaders promote an environment where everyone senses being listened to, valued, and acknowledged.

The more I dug into this topic, the more leaders I discovered who had tapped into the power of silence and witnessed unbelievable transformations within their teams. Take Jason Roberts, a manager at a global financial company, for example. He starts every team meeting with a moment of silence. Yes, that is right. He tells his team to ditch the distractions, clear their minds, and focus like nobody's business. That simple act of mindfulness brings on a wave of purpose and clarity that screams productivity and job satisfaction.

Then there is Maria Silva, the fearless leader of a nonprofit organization. She takes silence to a whole new level by organizing "silent retreats" - a whole day devoted to self-reflection and introspection. Meditation, journaling, silent walks - you name it, they do it. Maria realized that these moments of silence not only recharge her team but also create a deep bond between team members, resulting in a harmonious and effective working relationship.

When you incorporate the moments of silence into your working life, it creates a space of trust and openness where your team experiences comfort in expressing their ideas and concerns. And you know what happens next? Collaboration and innovation explode like fireworks on a get-together day!

So, in conclusion, do not underestimate the power of silence in leadership. By embracing silence, you are creating an environment that nurtures creativity, sharpens decision-making, and forges incredible connections with your team. Incorporate silence into your leadership practices to inspire and motivate in a noisy world.

Silence and Emotional Intelligence

Let me tell you about this gentleman. We will call him Mark. Mark was a big shot senior manager at this IT company, in charge of an entire team of talented folks. But he did struggle with emotions, both his own and his team members.

I still remember the first time I saw Mark in action during a meeting with his team. He just could not stop talking, giving no one else a chance to speak up. And his body language? Let us just say eye rolls, dismissive gestures, and zero empathy were his go-to moves. Tense silence filled the room, preventing his team from speaking or sharing ideas.

Understanding the value of emotional intelligence in effective leadership, I had a discussion with Mark about his communication style. I wanted to show him how silence can be a powerful tool for reflection and listening to others. I communicated to him that through creating moments of silence, he could foster a workplace where everyone sensed inclusion and understanding.

Mark did not believe in the idea. He could not comprehend the impact of staying silent. So, I had to hit him with some research that backed up the role of silence in developing emotional intelligence.

Studies have shown that silence gives us a chance to look inward and reflect on our emotions. Moments of silence prompt Mark to pause and examine his feelings. It helped him realize the impact his words and actions had on others, and he managed his emotions better.

Self-reflection and listening to others are both integral aspects of silence. In a noisy world, it is difficult to listen without interrupting or judging. So, I suggested Mark incorporate moments of silence into his conversations and meetings. And guess what? It worked! The silence fostered an environment where his team members felt acknowledged and appreciated. It deepened their understanding of each other and improved how they worked together.

And let us not forget about empathy, a crucial part of emotional intelligence. Silence gave Mark the chance to listen to his team members and understand where they were coming from. He realized that everyone's opinions and experiences mattered, and that created this culture of respect within his team.

Mark's leadership style changed. The moments of silence he brought into his communication not only helped him manage his own emotions, but they also encouraged his team to speak up. The meetings became more collaborative, with everyone engaging and coming up with innovative solutions. It was amazing to witness, and you could see the positive impact it had on the team's productivity and happiness.

Silence goes beyond being the absence of noise, but rather a state of being fully present and attuned to the moment. It was way to quiet the mind to let go of worries and distractions and truly connect with oneself and the world around. It is a strategic choice that can level up your emotional intelligence. It gives you the time and space to reflect, listen, and empathize. As leaders and individuals, we got to embrace the power of silence and see how it can transform our relationships, our teams, and even ourselves.

In summary, silence goes beyond being devoid of sound. It is a significant change with emotional intelligence. Through silence, we can foster self-reflection, active listening, and genuine empathy. By incorporating moments of silence into our interactions, we create a space that encourages open communication, collaboration, and emotional well-being. So, let us embrace the power of silence and watch how it can make a real difference in both our personal and professional lives.

Creating Silence-Friendly Workspaces

In today's world, everything moves at lightning speed. In today's world, we experience constant connection and bombardment with noise from every direction. Phones ringing, office spaces bustling—it is enough to make your head spin. As someone who explores the topic of silence, I recognize the powerful impact it has on our well-being and productivity.

Silence encompasses more than the lack of noise. It is a state of inner calm, a gentle tranquillity that clears our minds and helps us focus. Think of it as a secret weapon for unlocking our creativity and potential. In a world of noise and chaos, finding silence is a challenge. And that is why we need silence-friendly workspaces more than ever in today's bustling corporate jungle.

A silence-friendly workspace is a sacred place, a sanctuary where productivity flourishes, creativity blossoms, and well-being thrives. It is an environment that encourages silence, deep focus, and the work that makes your soul sing. How can we create such a space? Here are some practical tips and techniques:

First, designate quiet zones. These are places in the office where noise goes to die. A small space or room offers employees a peaceful retreat. No loud conversations, no phone calls yelling over each other, and no noisy office equipment. By having these designated zones, employees have a special place to dive deep into their work and unleash their inner ninja of concentration and productivity.

Second, bring out the big guns: noise-cancelling technology. Invest in some fancy noise-cancelling headphones or soundproofing materials and watch the distractions vanish. These magical headphones work wonders in open-plan offices where distractions are as common as pigeons in the city square. They block out all those background noises and let employees focus on their tasks, leading to higher productivity.

Third, let us implement a "quiet hours" policy. Dedicated time periods during the workday, where silence reigns supreme. No unnecessary conversations, no phone calls that could wake the dead. Just pure, uninterrupted silence. During these periods, employees can buckle down and tackle important tasks, brainstorm like mad scientists, or dive deep into contemplative work. Let the magic happen with no interruptions.

Now, let us talk about nature. Incorporating natural elements into the workspace is like inviting Mother Nature in for a cup of tea. Research has shown that being around nature increases our cognitive function and general sense of well-being. So, let us bring in some indoor plants, use natural materials, and give employees a glimpse of the great outdoors. We can even go a step further and design the workspace with biophilia principles—natural lighting, water features, and soothing colours that whisk us away to a peaceful oasis. The office feels serene, like a Zen Garden, rather than tense like a war zone.

Next up, mindfulness. It is trending, and rightfully so. Mindfulness techniques like meditation and deep breathing exercises help us find inner calm amidst the external uproar. So, why not encourage employees to practice mindfulness? Give them dedicated spaces or quiet corners where they can escape the chaos and focus on finding their centre. It is like hitting the reset button on their minds, creating a more focused and peaceful atmosphere.

But let us not forget about digital distractions. Silence is not just physical; it is also digital. So, let us establish clear communication guidelines. We can limit the use of emails or messaging apps for non-urgent matters and encourage face-to-face interactions for important discussions. By doing so, we reduce the digital noise and create a quieter space where employees can maintain their flow and concentration.

Creating silence-friendly workspaces is not just a fad; it is an absolute necessity in our modern work environment. By following these practical tips and techniques, employers can cultivate an environment that supports employee well-being, boosts productivity, and fosters a deeper connection between oneself and others. So, let us embrace the power of silence and discover the immense benefits it brings to our lives and work as we embark on this journey towards a quieter and more balanced workplace.

CHAPTER 3

Silence in Familial Relationships

Silence and Active Presence

You know, it is funny how life works. For example, noise would surround anyone growing up in a Mumbai city. The hustle and bustle of the city became the soundtrack of the existence. But you appreciate the power of silence when settle in a quieter town.

I remember going back home for visits and realizing that my family and I found the most meaningful moments in the quiet spaces. We shared an unspoken language, a connection that transcended words.

The understanding became even more important when I entered the corporate world. In my role as a project manager, I engaged with people from different walks of life. True communication goes beyond just talking. It is about those rare moments when the room goes quiet and fostering connections among everyone present happen at a deeper level.

In a world that is so focused on material success, we often forget that our loved ones just want our presence. They crave our undivided attention, to know that we are there. I realised this firsthand when my dad got sick. While next to him, grasping his hand, no words were necessary. It was the silent support that spoke volumes, that showed him I was there for him.

Being present applies beyond tough moments. It is for every day. When we try to be there with our loved ones, magic happens. We create a space where connections can flourish. We get to see and hear them in a way that words cannot capture.

In my book, I share stories of everyday people who have embraced the power of silence in their own lives. Vismaya, a working mom who struggled to balance it all. But she began setting aside daily time to be present with her kids. It made the difference. Her undivided attention became a channel for her children to open up and share, knowing she was listening.

These stories emphasize that the silence is inclusive. It does not matter who you are or what you are experiencing. By embracing silence, we can create deeper connections and find a sense of peace and purpose in our relationships.

Silence transcends barriers like a universal language. It encourages us to escape the noise and chaos and to find true understanding. Prioritize silence, presence, and genuine connections to create a world where we treasure them above all else.

Silence in Parenting

I got to say, silence is one of a parenting tool that often gets overlooked. Pondering about parenting in a noisy and chaotic world is a challenge. Once you harness the power of silence, it is a game-changer. Not only does it bring harmony to the family, but also strengthens the bond between you and your kids.

Taking inspiration from personal experience, active listening is vital to this entire parenting journey. It is easy to get caught up in everyday chaos and miss what our little ones are saying. But when we practice silence, we create this space for our kids to express themselves in their own unique ways.

Active listening goes beyond hearing what they say. It is about paying attention to their emotions, their body language, and those unspoken needs. We shut off our own thoughts and give our undivided attention to our kids. We not only show them we value their opinions and feelings, but we also open the door for the real heart-to-heart conversations and deeper connections.

Now, let us talk about setting boundaries. It is important for children to understand the boundaries of acceptable behaviour. And it is up to us parents to guide them in figuring that out. A moment of silence can prevent us from reacting, rather respond in a calm and thoughtful way.

When conflicts arise, it is common for emotions to intensify, leading to outbursts of anger or frustration. But silence acts like a buffer, giving us the space to evaluate the situation and respond with the self-control. Pausing not only shows to our children the repercussions of actions, but it also maintains a secure and supportive environment.

Now let us get to open communication, the foundation of any healthy relationship. As parents, we got to create an environment where our kids can express themselves with no fear of judgement. But sometimes, our knee-jerk reaction is to jump in and solve their problems. Embracing silence in these moments creates a safe space for our kids to express their thoughts, emotions, and concerns, experiencing no sense of urgency or interruption.

By staying silent and just letting our kids spill their hearts out, we are not only validating their experiences, but we are also giving them a chance to flex their problem-solving muscles. It is empowering them to think and make those informed decisions. It helps them build independence and self-confidence.

In my parenting journey, I have seen firsthand the transformative power of silence. I have learned that it is unnecessary for me to always offer answers or solutions when my child comes to me with their problems. Sometimes, all they need is a listening ear and someone to be present as they process their thoughts and emotions.

Silence in parenting does not imply a lack of care or disconnection. It is about creating an environment where our kids experience being heard, understood, and respected. It is about building trust and connection so that open and honest communication can thrive.

But I want to clarify that using silence as a parenting tool is not one-size-fits-all. Each kid is unique and needs different support and guidance. We got to adapt and customize our approach based on what our kids need most.

It is uncomfortable to incorporate moments of silence in our parenting, in a society that prioritizes constant stimulation and immediate satisfaction. By embracing silence, we can cultivate peace, purpose, and connection that will help us and our children in the future.

So, here is to finding those moments of silence during this chaotic parenting journey. Let us show our kids the importance of embracing silence, and let us lead by example, cultivating this practice within ourselves. May we have the courage to seek moments of silence amidst the noise, and may we discover the profound peace, purpose, and connection that comes with it. Cheers!

Silence and Conflict Resolution

Okay, folks, let us talk about using silence to handle family conflicts. But before we begin, let us clarify what silence signifies in this context. It is not sitting there making no tempted noise. It is a purposeful decision not to blabber away. You can choose to listen, see, and let the unspoken words do the talking.

So, in resolving conflicts within the family, silence is a significant change. Our first instinct might be to go all word-vomit, trying to prove our point or defend ourselves. But that just makes things worse. Both sides become stubborn and entrenched. But if we embrace silence as a strategy, we create an environment that is open to understanding and finding a resolution.

One of the main tricks to using silence in conflict resolution is active listening. This requires paying attention to both the words and non-verbal cues. You know, body language, tone of voice, facial expressions. When we show we are listening, we are showing respect for the other person's point of view. And that makes for healthy communication and mutual understanding.

During difficult moments at home, remember that the goal is not to win the argument. It is about finding common ground and making everyone happy. And that is where silence comes in. Instead of interrupting and pushing our own agenda, we can use silence to make room for others to express themselves. This creates a sense of inclusion and validation for them, while also granting us valuable understanding of their viewpoint.

When caught in the moment, we often have the urge to speak without thinking. But hold up! Silence offers the opportunity to pause and contemplate our emotions and intentions. Let our words seek resolution, not self-justification. Opting for a brief break, selecting silence over a hasty response, aids in avoiding uttering hurtful words that we will later repent. It is silence that sets the stage for a more thoughtful and productive conversation.

Another genius way to use silence in conflict resolution is through mindfulness. It means being present, without judgment or fixation on the outcome. By practicing mindfulness during conflicts, we become more aware of our own emotional reactions and those of others. And that awareness? It allows us to respond with empathy and compassion, instead of jumping into attack mode.

When things are super tensed and emotions are running wild, silence can be a pressure-release valve. Sometimes, when we step back and choose silence, it stops things from getting even uglier. Silence offers a tranquil moment for reflection, without words.

Attaining a state of calmness is crucial for both parties to approach the conflict.

Here are the incredible stories I have encountered. They prove just how powerful silence can be in resolving family conflicts. Take this husband and wife, for example. They were stuck in this never-ending cycle of fights and disagreements. Their lack of communication broke their trust and connection into a million pieces. But when they embraced silence, they listened to each other's pain and grievances. By creating a sacred silence, they gave themselves time to hear each other. They empathized and worked together to find a resolution that respected both their needs and desires.

Here is another story that hits you deep. A mom and daughter who had drifted apart went on a silent retreat. Days of silence helped them appreciate the power of unspoken words. In their shared silence, they found solace, understanding, and a newfound love for each other. They bridged the long-standing gap between them. It was a beautiful and healing experience.

These stories, along with many others, show us just how silence can transform family conflicts. Whether by active listening, reflecting, diffusing tension, or creating space for understanding, silence is a catalyst for change. When we make silence part of our conflict resolution strategy, we create healthier communication, understanding, and resolution in our families. In a world that's always too loud, silence is our secret weapon for finding peace, purpose, and connection.

As I keep exploring the power of silence, I am amazed by ordinary people who have turned their families around through unspoken words. It is these stories that remind us that conflicts—yes; they are bound to happen—are opportunities for growth, healing, and connection. By embracing silence and its transformative potential, we can build deeper relationships, nurture understanding, and create a home that is full of peace and love.

In the next chapter, we will go beyond family conflicts and see how silence can work its magic in our relationships with friends, colleagues, and even strangers. We will dig into how silence fosters empathy, builds bridges, and promotes teamwork. By employing stories and real-life examples, we will see the universal power of silence in fostering peace, purpose, and connection in our noisy world.

Silence and Forgiveness

The idea of silence and its incredible impact on our lives continues to fascinate me as I explore how we can use silence to help us in forgiving, heal, and rebuilding trust in our family relationships. It is a magical potion that breaks walls of resentment and pain, bringing us closer.

Anyone growing up in a tight-knit family in India would have seen it in family dynamics. From the unconditional love and support of parents to the occasional sibling spats, you would have seen how silence can either make or break our family ties. Silence has the potential to heal and strengthen family bonds, revealing its true power.

The journey towards forgiveness, healing, and trust starts with acknowledging the pain and hurt we experience. Sometimes, we get stuck in this never-ending cycle of blaming and holding grudges, unable to move forward. But when we embrace silence, when we listen to our own emotions and reflect on our actions, the process of forgiveness begins.

Silence gives us the space to examine ourselves and take responsibility for our own mistakes. In the absence of noise and distractions, we can delve into our thoughts and emotions, gaining deep clarity and understanding. It is like we develop this empathy towards ourselves and our loved ones, realizing their perspective and what motivated their actions.

The incredible thing about silence is how it can subdue our thirst for revenge and foster compassion instead. It helps us let go of our ego, the need to 'win' or be 'right,' and instead prioritize our relationships with our family. In silence, we learn the art of deep listening, healing the pain, anger, and regret that are hidden beneath the surface.

Through research, I have come across the jaw-dropping stories of people who have used the power of silence to heal and rebuild trust within their families. One of these stories is about Vishesh and his dad, Rajesh.

Vishesh's relationship with his dad was always rocky, filled with misunderstandings and hurtful actions. Tired of the tension, Vishesh sought solace and clarity in a peaceful countryside cottage. It was in this blissful silence that Vishesh realized the weight of his anger towards his dad and how it was affecting his own well-being.

Days went by, and Vishesh thought about why their relationship had gone south. He understood his dad's own struggles and insecurities, which often led to his hurtful behaviour. In the comforting embrace of silence, Vishesh confronted his own vulnerabilities, realizing that his own actions had contributed to the toxic dynamic between them.

With a newfound sense of compassion and forgiveness, Vishesh reached out to his dad. He invited him to join him in a space of genuine connection and honest conversation. Together, they acknowledged their past mistakes and apologized for the pain they had caused each other. Through the power of silence, Vishesh and Rajesh transformed from adversaries to vulnerable, empathetic beings.

Stories of Vishesh and Rajesh's show us that silence is not about hiding our emotions or avoiding confrontation. It is about creating a space for healing and connection. It is about healing of our own wounds with self-compassion and extending that same compassion to our loved ones.

When individuals embrace silence with intention and support it with open communication, they create a mighty tool for rebuilding trust in family relationships. It provides a safe and judgement-free environment for everyone to express themselves. In this space, true healing happens as we acknowledge past hurts and work towards forgiveness and understanding.

And silence does not just help us heal our family bonds, it helps us grow as individuals within these relationships. When we navigate the complexities of family dynamics, silence gives us the chance for introspection. We can find and discuss our own patterns of behaviour that keep fuelling the conflicts. By growing and reflecting on ourselves, we contribute to the healing and strengthening of our family ties.

In closing this chapter, I am reminded of the wise words of Mahatma Gandhi, who said, "In the silence, the soul finds the path in a clearer light, and what is elusive and deceptive resolves itself into crystal clearness." Silence guides us towards forgiveness, healing, and trust within our families. We release the past and embrace renewed connections and love. It is as rare as finding a unicorn or a pot of gold.

Creating Silent Spaces at Home

You know what is crazy? It is as elusive as a unicorn or a pot of gold. That is right, I am talking about finding silence in your own home. I mean, a struggle. There is constant noise everywhere, from the blaring TV to the annoying beeping of your smartphone. It appears a mission is impossible, but fear not! I have got tips that might just help you create those silent spaces you crave.

Choose a specific area in your home as a "quiet zone" as the first step. Whatever floats your boat. Creating a specific area for solace is essential in attaining inner peace. The household is a sacred space for silence and reflection, creating a touch of magic in the air.

But wait, there is more! You got to set the boundaries and expectations for noise levels in your home. Make a mental note of the specified time and location for activities. I call it the "quiet hour" and is a significant change. Imagine everyone in the household turning off electronics and engaging in quiet activities, say, reading or journaling. It is like a symphony of tranquillity.

Now, let us tackle those pesky external noises. Soundproofing is the name of the game. Add rugs or curtains to absorb sound, or invest in soundproofing materials for a more comprehensive solution. Either way, by shutting out the outside world, you create a serene oasis of calmness within your humble abode.

Before we go ahead, we must discuss internal sources of noise. Yes, I am talking about clutter and disorganization. Trust me, like a tornado of chaos that makes it impossible to find any moments of silence. So, get rid of the clutter, organize your stuff, and streamline your routines. It is like clearing the path to tranquillity.

And here is a radical idea: create a technology-free zone in your home. Technology is a noisy neighbour. So, make some areas or times in your home off-limits for technology. By disconnecting from those devices, you can reconnect with yourself and your loved ones.

Okay, now let us talk about the fun stuff. You got to create an atmosphere of relaxation and tranquillity in your silent spaces. Think soothing colours, cozy furniture, and calming decor. Picture this: plants, soft lighting, and gentle scents wafting through the air. It is like a spa in your own home. This environment offers peace and reminds us to slow down and embrace silence.

Yet, creating silent spaces involves more than just physical silence. It is also about finding emotional and mental silence. To achieve this, one must be mindful and live in the present. Try meditation, take deep breaths, or jot down your thoughts in a journal. Trust me, it is like a volume knob for your mind.

Creating silent spaces at home is like discovering a hidden treasure in a noisy world. It takes some effort, but it is worth it. Designating quiet zones, setting boundaries, soundproofing, decluttering, and creating a peaceful atmosphere, all while practicing mindfulness - it is the secret recipe for peace, purpose, and connection in your everyday life. So, go on and create your own silent sanctuary.

CHAPTER 4

Silence in Personal Relationships

Silence and Connection

Silence. Many people use the word, but they often overlook its true power. In a noisy world filled with distractions, embracing silence can deepen connections with others.

I have observed it both in my life and in the lives of regular people I have met. There have been countless moments where silence has played a huge role in strengthening the bonds of love and friendship. And that is something special.

Let us start with romantic relationships. You know, in a society where we rely on words to express wish, affection and love, silence can seem like it is lacking, like it is empty. Delving deeper, one discovers that silence speaks louder than words.

Picture a serene moment with your partner, relishing each other's company in silence. You are sitting there, absorbing each other's presence. Beyond words, in that peaceful moment, there is an unspoken awareness, a profound sense of comfort and connection. True intimacy thrives in moments of silence, when words are unnecessary. Love simply flows, with no language barriers holding it back.

I remember this couple, Sarah, and James. They knew they lost that silent connection they had, so they made it their mission to rekindle that fire. Their successful reconnection involved escaping to a remote cabin.

Next to each other, they sat and watched the sunset, holding hands in complete silence. It was not just silence, their souls seemed in sync. In that quiet moment, they found a deeper connection beyond their daily routines. It reminded them of their genuine love for each other.

Silence in a relationship can also mean being vulnerable with each other. When you allow yourself to be silent, you create this safe space for your partner to be their true selves. Grasping each other's perspectives occurs, with no filters or pretences.

Let me give you an example. A couple named Anna and Michael have been together for a while. They found that the silence they shared in moments of vulnerability brought them even closer. It is like in those quiet moments; they peeled back all the layers of fear, insecurity, and dreams, and they just bared their souls to each other. It is a connection that nothing can break. They do not fear judgment or rejection because of the silence.

Friendships benefit from the power of silence, too. In a noisy world filled with constant chatter, sitting in silence with a friend shows a deep level of trust and strength in the relationship. It is like conveying, "I am content with just being here with you and no words are necessary."

Mark and Samantha, childhood friends, share a special bond. As they grew up and faced the craziness of adulting, they found comfort in their silence. They knew that even without words, their bond was solid. Each silent moment they shared spoke volumes about their unwavering support for each other.

Do not mistake silence for a complete absence of communication. It is the opposite. Silence creates this space for deeper communication to happen. It makes you listen and understand the unspoken feelings and thoughts of the people you care about.

Studies even show that silence helps promote empathy and compassion in relationships. When you take a pause and listen, you are creating an environment where your loved ones feel heard and validated. In that state of quiet presence, you can connect on a whole different level. It is like forging this unbreakable bond that transcends words.

Silence is like its own language, one that speaks straight to the heart and soul. It is this bridge that connects us to others, letting us build relationships that are not just built on words alone. In silence, we find peace, purpose, and, most importantly, connection—that is what it means to be human.

In your journey of embracing silence in relationships, remember that it is not something to fear or avoid. Let it work its magic and you will discover a world of connection and intimacy that is beyond your wildest dreams.

In the next chapter, we are going to dive even deeper into how silence can transform our relationship with ourselves. It is all about uncovering those hidden treasures within us. In the meantime, pause and appreciate the silence. Let it guide you to a deeper connection with the people you hold dear.

Silence and Boundaries

Imagine the vibrant chaos of growing up in Bangalore. The symphony of sounds is ever-present. The blaring horns of cars, the boisterous calls of street vendors, and the perpetual hustle and bustle become your constant companions. Little did I know, the absence of sound held an extraordinary power and beauty, waiting to be discovered.

Silence has this uncanny ability to transcend words and bring us closer to our deepest selves. It is in those moments of hushed reflection that our true essence shines through and we gain a profound understanding of who we are and what we need. And in those moments that we can show and honour our personal boundaries, ensuring our own well-being.

Boundaries are the foundation of any healthy relationship, whether with ourselves or with others. Without boundaries, we find ourselves at the mercy of others, allowing them to dictate our emotions and actions. It is a recipe for resentment, exhaustion, and losing our very identity.

But setting boundaries is not as simple as snapping our fingers. It is an art that requires not just honest communication, but a deep self-awareness and the willingness to honour our own needs. And that is where the tremendous power of silence comes into play.

Silence becomes a masterful tool in boundary-setting because it grants us the precious time and space to reflect on our feelings and needs before responding. Pausing for a moment of silence aids me in evaluating if a request aligns with my values and priorities.

Just, a dear friend asked me to join him on a committee for a cause he was passionate about. An immediate sense of obligation washed over me because of the weight of our long-standing friendship. But I entered the realm of silence and introspection, questioning if this new commitment would fit into my already jam-packed schedule and resonate with my personal values.

In that fleeting instance of tranquillity, I came to realize that while I respected my friend's enthusiasm, I did not have the bandwidth to immerse myself in the cause. I recognized that my well-being and self-care needed to be front and centre. So instead of submitting to his ask, I declined, explaining my reasons, and offering alternative means of support.

Understanding this practice of incorporating silence to set up and honour personal boundaries leads to remarkable outcomes, not only for self-awareness but for the thriving of relationships. When we communicate and assert our boundaries, we grant others the opportunity to understand our needs and expectations, thus paving the way for mutual respect and understanding.

Of course, employing silence to set boundaries does not mean we should be always mute. Rather, it is about using silence as an instrument of introspection and self-reflection before we articulate our boundaries and communicate them to others.

Another pivotal piece of boundary-setting involves recognizing and honouring the boundaries of those around us. In the same way that we may delineate our own limits, we extend that same courtesy to our fellow humans. This calls for attentive listening and empathizing with their needs and boundaries.

As human beings, we weave our lives together, and our words and actions hold tremendous weight. Silence, coupled with mindfulness, allows us to grasp the impact our choices can have on those around us. It is only when we conscientiously embrace silence, we avoid overstepping the boundaries of others and cultivate empathy and compassion.

I recall an instance when a colleague was grappling with a personal crisis. He wore his turbulence on his sleeve, distraught and unable to cope. Instead of bombarding him with questions and unsolicited advice, I sat beside him in silence, offering my presence and support without uttering a single word.

Within that pregnant pause, I recognized the importance of honouring his need for space, of providing a support to process his emotions. It was not about playing superhero or coming up with quick fixes; it was about giving him the room to unburden himself if he so desired, while respecting his boundaries.

By embracing the power of silence in this way, we cultivate a profound empathy and compassion for others, fostering a more harmonious and supportive environment for everyone involved.

Taking part in the practice of utilizing silence to establish and uphold personal boundaries is not always straightforward in a world that bombards us with noise and incessant demands. But, if we are intentional about carving out moments of silence in our lives, we create sanctuaries for self-reflection, self-awareness, and self-care.

In conclusion, silence has the potential to metamorphose in our lives if we will embrace and harness its power. By employing silence to show and respect personal boundaries, we deepen our self-awareness, strengthen our relationships, and foster a climate of mutual respect and understanding. It is through periods of silence that we discover peace, purpose, and connection amidst the deafening clamour of the world.

Silence and Vulnerability

I was interested in delving into the idea of silence. This college library suggests a link between silence in relationships and vulnerability. When we stop talking, we can open up and connect on a deeper level. And that hit home for me.

I recall a time when a couple experienced difficulties in their relationship. They struggled to communicate, feeling out of sync. They shared a moment of silence, sitting there without uttering a word. And it was like the walls between them started crumbling.

In the silence, they contemplated their emotions undisturbed. It was intense. They realized that their fights and arguments were just hiding their own insecurities and fears. And once they embraced that vulnerability, they had this deep, authentic conversation that brought them closer together and helped them heal.

But this couple is not alone in their experience. Other individuals have experienced similar situations. This one couple mentioned how silent walks in nature helped them connect in a whole new way. Their silent presence fostered vulnerability between them. It created this safe space where they could open up.

So, I wanted to dig deeper. I started checking out spiritual traditions and they have been talking about the power of silence. In meditation, silence is the key to self-discovery. When you sit in silence and just observe your thoughts and feelings with no judgement, you can tap into your true self and connect with who you are.

Zen master Thich Nhat Hanh said it best, "Silence is crucial for listening to ourselves. It is in that quiet that we can realize our deepest emotions and fears." It is so true, right? Being aware simplifies embracing vulnerability and accepting oneself with love and kindness.

So, armed with this insight, I started bringing silence into my conversations. Instead of filling the awkward pauses, I let them hang and gave myself and the other person time to think and reflect. It differed. Instead of just chatting surface-level stuff, we dug deeper and connected on a whole new level.

I stayed silent and offer a presence for him instead of giving advice or comforting words. And guess what? In that quietness, he experienced a sense of security that allowed him to express and show his innermost challenges and anxieties. It was powerful. It reminded me of how silence can create a space for vulnerability and authentic connection.

Silence is more than just quiet. It is this incredible force that can lead to deep communication and emotional intimacy. When we embrace silence in our relationships, it gives vulnerability room to grow and allows each other to see and understand us. In this noisy world we live in, silence is like a secret weapon for finding peace, purpose, and connection in our relationships.

Silence does not occur on its own. We must try to cultivate it in our lives. Amidst chaos, we must find moments of stillness. It means facing our own vulnerability head-on and being open to listening to ourselves and others.

In a world that tries to shut vulnerability down and rewards constant noise, it is crucial that we honour the power of silence and make it a part of our lives and relationships. Whether taking silent walks, sitting in meditation, or creating space in our conversations, silence has this incredible ability to unlock our innermost selves and create a space of safety and authenticity. In that space, we can form genuine connections and discover the peace and purpose we seek.

Silence and Conflict Resolution

During my childhood in a village in India, my parents reminded me that being silent was a virtue. My parents would drill it into my head to think before I spoke, to listen to others, and to appreciate the magic of silence. Little did I realize, the wisdom I gained would shape my life and understanding of resolving conflicts.

On my journey through various jobs and personal relationships, I realize that silence is not just this secret weapon for resolving conflicts; it is the key ingredient for empathy and healthy communication. When we learn to embrace the power of silence, it opens a world of possibilities. It allows us to listen, to understand different perspectives, and to find common ground even when we seem worlds apart.

One trick to using silence as a conflict resolution tool is to practice active listening. We experience an onslaught of information and distractions in today's crazy and noisy world. The need to be heard and prove ourselves can consume us in arguments. To find a resolution, we must practice silence and attentive listening. That is when we will understand their needs and wants, and it is the first step towards creating empathy and compassion.

In my personal relationships, I have discovered that hitting pause and embracing silence during conflicts can be game-changing. It gives both parties a chance to take a breath, gather their thoughts, and approach the situation from a rational and understanding standpoint. By creating a space of silence, we create an environment where both sides can speak without interruption, allowing for more openness and honesty.

Another trick for using silence in conflict resolution is to practice mindfulness. Mindfulness means being present in the moment, without judgment or attachment. When we cultivate this practice, we become more aware of our own thoughts and emotions during conflicts, as well as the impact of our words and actions on the other person.

When faced with a conflict, taking a moment of silence to practice mindfulness can help us gain a deeper understanding of our own reactions and triggers. By focusing on our breath, observing our thoughts, and grounding ourselves in the present moment, we approach the conflict with a calm and centred mindset. This allows us to respond rather than react, and to communicate our thoughts and feelings in a more constructive and respectful way.

Silence can work wonders for promoting healthy communication in our personal relationships. In this fast-paced world we live in, constant messages, notifications, and distractions bombard us. Unfortunately, that noise drowns out the important conversations that need to happen. So, we must create moments of silence in our relationships to enable deep and meaningful communication.

One way to incorporate silence into our relationships is to establish check-ins or quiet times. These intentional moments involve both parties agreeing to remove distractions, sit in silence, and be present with each other. Believe me, this intentional silence creates an environment where a genuine sense of connection and understanding can emerge.

On top of that, silence is a powerful tool for self-reflection and self-expression. By taking the time to be silent and tap into our inner thoughts and emotions, we gain a better understanding of ourselves and our own needs. This self-awareness enables us to communicate our thoughts, desires, and boundaries more effectively, resulting in healthier and more fulfilling relationships.

To conclude, silence is not an empty void waiting to be filled, but a powerful tool waiting to be embraced. By practicing active listening, mindfulness, and incorporating moments of silence in our personal relationships, we can resolve conflicts, foster empathy, and promote healthy communication. The stories of ordinary folks who have overcome challenges shared in this book serve as proof of the transformative power of silence. Let us embrace silence and foster meaningful connections in this noisy world.

Embracing Silence Together

In this chaotic, fast-paced world we live in, discovering moments of silence and stillness can seem like attempting to catch a break in a thunderstorm. We face distractions - smartphones buzz incessantly, notifications flood. We experience a sense of being connected, always on, and causing us being overwhelmed and disconnected. Choose a regular time to block out external distractions and give each other undivided attention.

Amid chaos, a secret weapon can bring us peace, purpose, and connection. It is called silence. Yes, I know, it sounds simple, but trust me, it is powerful.

Let us discuss the importance of embracing silence in relationships during our chat. When we invite moments of silence into our lives with our partners and friends, we can strengthen our bonds, grow together, and create a sacred space for deep conversations.

Now, I get that this might sound daunting, especially if you and your loved ones are used to non-stop chatter and stimulation. Just hold on for a second. With a bit of patience, practice, and the right mindset, you can create an environment where silence becomes a treasure in your relationship.

Here are a few practical exercises and activities you can give a whirl:

Let us turn off the noise. Pause and recognize the sources of noise in your life - the blaring TV, the social media frenzy, and the constant urge to talk. Schedule dedicated moments to disconnect from distractions and focus on each other. It could be as simple as sitting in silence for a sweet 15 minutes every evening, giving yourselves a chance to unwind and simply... be.

Next up, nature walks. Mother Nature has this incredible power to calm the restless soul and create a peaceful atmosphere. So, plan regular outings with your family or friends to soak up some of that magic. The key is to embrace the silence. Let the sounds of nature weave their melody between you. Take in the beauty around you and let nature guide your thoughts and emotions.

Now, let us get zen. Meditation, my friend. Trust me, it is a game-changer. Find a quiet place where you can both sit, cross-legged or in chairs - whatever floats your boat. Close your eyes, take a deep breath, and let your thoughts settle. Focus on your breath, and do your best to let go of distractions. By meditating together, you are creating this shared space of stillness where you connect on a whole another level.

And how about that good old journaling? Involving oneself in writing can act as an efficient means of introspection and individual advancement. So, set aside some time each week where you and your partner or friends can journal in silence. Find a peaceful spot, grab your journals, and let your thoughts flow onto the pages. Afterwards, if you are sensing it, you can choose to share and discuss your reflections. Or you can keep them between you and your journal. That is cool too. Understand that this activity enables you to delve into your inner world and form connections through vulnerability.

Now, let us tackle the tech. We are all addicted to our devices, right? It makes us feel disconnected from the people right in front of us. of us. So, here is what I propose: tech-free evenings. Disconnect from gadgets and engage in activities that foster real connections and tranquillity. Maybe cook up a delicious meal together, play some board games, or sit on the porch and marvel at the sunset without a word. The magic lies in the silence.

And the big thing - silent retreats. I know, I know, it might sound intense, but hear me out. A silent retreat offers you and your loved ones this magical opportunity to disconnect from the outside world and dive headfirst into silence. It could be a weekend getaway, a week-long adventure - whatever floats your boat. The point is, when you embrace silence in a structured environment, it can have a crazy profound impact on your relationship.

Now, I want to make one thing clear: when we talk about embracing silence together, we are not saying you should give up on conversation altogether. No! about finding those moments of stillness where deeper connections can unfold. In those silences, we learn to listen - not to the words being spoken, but to the unspoken emotions and desires of our loved ones.

A brief story to bring it all together. There was this couple, Rashmi, and Vivaan. Married for over 25 years, they took pride in their strong communication skills. Noise overtook but as their careers got more demanding and their kids grew older, that is until they made a conscious decision to embrace silence together.

They started with those tech-free evenings we talked about. They rediscovered the joy of cooking together, engaging in deep conversations without the distraction of devices. Over time, they incorporated nature walks and meditation into their routine. They found solace in the beauty of nature and within themselves.

Slowly but surely, Rashmi and Vivaan experienced a profound shift in their relationship. Those moments of silence allowed them to understand each other's needs, desires, and fears. They learned words were not always necessary to communicate love and support. Silence and an embrace speak volumes.

Involving in moments of silence together demands effort, commitment, and a readiness to explore your connection with your partner or friends. It is strange and uncomfortable. But the rewards? They are priceless. And as you journey through the exercises, I have shared with you, remember this: silence has the power to transform and heal. By embracing it together, you create space for growth, connection, and the discovery of a profound inner peace that ripples out into every corner of your life.

CHAPTER 5

Personal Growth and Transformation

Silence and Self-Reflection

You know, throughout history, there have been these wise people from different cultures and spiritual backgrounds. Who were the ones who thought, "Silence is key!" On Socrates, he maintained that a life without examination is meaningless. The Buddha taught the timeless wisdom of silence and self-reflection, urging people to sit and listen.

But let us be real here. In our modern society, silence is this rare unicorn. Everywhere we turn, noise fills our lives - smartphones buzzing, the TV blaring, and the traffic that never seems to stop. We have lost touch with the beauty and potential of silence. But listen up, my friend, we can get it back. We have the power to reclaim this treasure and use it to change our lives.

When we embrace silence and make it a regular thing in our lives, we open a whole new world of self-discovery. Without the distractions, we can listen to that little voice inside our heads. You know, the one that knows what we want and what we fear. Through self-reflection, we find the courage to face and conquer our doubts and insecurities. Ignoring preconceptions and external pressures empowers us to discover our genuine identities.

Silence helps us figure out what matters to us. In a loud world, we easily succumb to others' opinions and societal pressures. Without reflecting on our values, we may pursue goals that do not align with them. But with silence, we can reassess our priorities and figure out what matters to us. This self-reflection lets us make choices that make us happy and fulfilled.

Plus, silence helps us become more self-aware. In our fast-paced world, we rarely reflect on our thoughts, feelings, and actions. Creating moments of silence allows us to align with our thoughts and identify constraining patterns. We can recognize negative thought patterns and beliefs and change them for the better. It is a superpower, giving us a better understanding of ourselves and helping us grow and develop.

Silence becomes our compass in pursuing self-discovery and transformation. When we retreat from the noise and distractions, we find a sanctuary where we can connect with our inner selves and tap into our own wisdom. We find the answers to our deepest questions and uncover our hidden potential. Silence guides us towards a life that is aligned with our true values and aspirations.

From my experience, I must say, silence is amazing. The search for moments of calm and silence has granted me a clear perspective on life. I have discovered my priorities, set goals, and determined the steps to achieve them. In moments of silence, I discovered the determination to overcome challenges and pursue my dreams. By practicing silence, I have become more self-aware, connected with myself and others, and found peace and purpose in a chaotic world.

So, my friend, I want to invite you on this journey of silence and self-reflection. Set aside time each day to disconnect from distractions and connect with your inner self. Let the power of silence guide you towards self-discovery, purpose, and peace. Trust me, it is a game-changer.

Silence and Mindset

I got to tell you; silence used to be this mysterious thing for me. Like this empty void where nothing was happening. But I was wrong. Silence can alter our thoughts and feelings. In this crazy world we live in, with all its noise and distractions, silence can be a total game-changer.

I never paid much attention to silence before. I mean, I was always into facts and problem-solving, living in my logical little bubble. Everything changed when I started dabbling in mindfulness and meditation. I realized that silence had this enormous impact on my mindset and my outlook on life.

See, silence gives you this space to think and reflect. In a state of silence, you have a personal bubble where you can delve into thoughts and emotions without external distractions. Pause and explore your feelings, uncover the reasons behind them, including any obstacles or burdens.

Once you pay attention to those inner struggles, silence has this crazy power to help you change your perspective and start seeing things in a more positive light. It is like you can challenge all those negative thoughts and replace them with brighter, more empowering ones. Embrace the silence to shed limiting beliefs and open yourself to growth, believing in your ability to overcome anything.

Silence strengthens you. It also has incredible benefits for your overall well-being. Amidst the buzzing world, we often neglect signifying inner calm. Silence lets you tap into your inner strength and find that sense of peace and stability that you need. It is like hitting the reset button for your mind, body, and soul.

And get this, science backs it up! Studies show that silence can activate different parts of your brain that handle creativity and problem-solving. It is like your brain's little secret weapon. Plus, that quiet time reduces your stress and improves your sleep, which is like the building blocks of a healthy life.

But you know the best part? Silence brings you closer to yourself and the surrounding people. Amid the chaos, silence helps you tap into your intuition, that gut feeling that guides you towards what is important. It makes you more self-aware and connected to your true self. And that connection? It spills out to the people in your life, strengthening your relationships and making you feel you belong.

So many people have experienced this transformation. There is this one man named Vikram, who was drowning in stress and burnout from his demanding job. But he took a break and explored the power of silence. And you know what he found? It was his mindset that was causing all his stress. He was always chasing perfection and fearing failure. But silence helped him see that progress mattered more than perfection, and that personal growth was where he would find true fulfilment.

Vikram's story is a shining example of how silence can change your life. Amid the noise, embracing silence lets you reconnect with yourself, find your purpose, and replace negative thoughts with positive ones. It builds resilience within you and opens doors to deeper connections with yourself and those around you.

So, silence is not merely an absence of noise. It has the power to transform your perspective on the world and yourself. It is not always easy to make space for it in your life, but it is worth it. When you embrace silence, you find peace, purpose, and connection in this crazy, noisy world. So, let us go on this journey together and unlock the power of silence within us.

Silence and Creativity

When I started digging into the total silence and creativity thing, I did not know the power it held. The ability to find peace in chaos is truly remarkable. I mean, think about it. Throughout history, these crazy smart people - philosophers, artists, musicians, writers - they all knew that silence was like their secret weapon. It fuelled their creativity, sparked innovative ideas, and took them on these wild journeys of imagination.

Yet, to explore the connection between silence and creativity, we must delve into the past. Ancient civilizations were onto something, you know. In ancient Greece, they had this thing called 'maieutic,' a Socratic method of teaching by question and answer- where philosophers like Socrates would just sit in silence for ages, encouraging deep thinking and reflection. It was like a portal to their inner wisdom and unleashed this flood of inspiration and ideas.

Fast forward to the Renaissance, it is like a whole explosion of art. Take people like Leonardo da Vinci. He possessed this secret sauce, and it was not the absence of noise. It was this state of mind, this silence within, that unlocked his creative genius. He once said, "A significant silence overcomes me, and my mind surges forth." Can you imagine feeling that?

The floodgates of creativity burst open when he stumbled upon that silence.

Same goes for the world of music. Johann Sebastian Bach. He embraced silence in his compositions, those moments they call 'rests.' The goal was to enhance the brilliance of those beautiful melodies through contrast, rather than taking a break. It was the silence that brought out the emotions and left audiences in awe.

Jump to the modern era, and silence has continued to evolve in its role. Marcel Proust, this French writer, he said something that stuck with me. Based on his perspective, genuine discovery does not involve finding new landscapes, but perceiving things with a fresh outlook. An open mindset that offered a fresh view of the world. And he did dive deep into his imagination. His words created these vibrant images and provided us with these distinct viewpoints.

We have Emily Dickinson, an American poet. For her, silence was like this magical world of plush soundlessness. She viewed it as a gateway to boundless creativity, allowing her imagination to roam free from the distractions of everyday life. She connected her poetry to those moments of silence, drawing inspiration from the whispers of her inner world.

Now, science even backs up this complete silence and creativity thing. Studies have shown that silence can boost our brain power, get those creative juices flowing, and stimulate the parts of our brain that handle introspection and imagination. In a noisy, distracting world, it is crucial to find moments of silence.

But why does silence have such a profound effect on our creativity? Well, perhaps it is because it allows our minds the opportunity to reflect. It is like a whole alternative universe waiting to be explored. Embracing silence helps us release expectations, judgments, and the pressure to conform. We can go on these wild thought adventures and allow our desires and emotions to guide us. Silence lets us listen to the whispers of our creative souls, all those ideas and inspiration that can shape our lives and the world.

For me, silence has been a game-changer. I used to be stuck in this noisy world, surrounded by the constant buzz of my job as an engineer and IT professional. But once I started seeking those moments of silence, through meditation and mindfulness, something shifted. It felt like a veil lifted, revealing a fresh perspective of the world. Impossible problems became conquerable mountains. In the silence, I discovered peace, purpose, and a connection to something greater than me.

I have read, many people who found the power of silence and used it to conquer challenges and achieve their dreams. They found that inner peace amidst the noise, and it let their creative spirit soar. Entrepreneurs with groundbreaking ideas, artists who created mind-blowing masterpieces - their stories are proof of how silence can change everything with creativity and innovation.

Silence goes beyond the mere absence of noise. It is this magical canvas, waiting for us to paint it with the colours of our imagination. It is in those quiet moments we tap into the depths of our creativity and unleash our limitless potential. By embracing silence, we can find peace, purpose, and connection in this noisy world. When we do that, we become part of something larger, leaving a mark on the tapestry of human existence.

Silence and Self-Care

In our crazy, fast-paced world, it is damn near impossible to find a moment of silence. I mean, our lives are like an unending circus of noise and distractions. Our attention is always in demand, from buzzing phones to chaotic traffic. And let us be real. We take a break to tune into our own thoughts and surroundings.

Exploring the concept of "power of silence," I realized it is about more than just ignoring the world. It is about utilizing silence as a tool for self-care, stress relief, and reconnecting with our own selves. Prepare yourself, as I guide you on incorporating silence into your daily routine to maximize its benefits.

Step one is all about carving out some space for silence in your life. Scheduling specific moments of silence can involve activities such as meditation, journaling, or stillness. By attempting to create this time, you are sending a loud and clear message to yourself that your well-being and inner peace matter.

After setting aside sacred time for silence, it is time to be present. See, a lot of us approach silence with the mindset of shutting everything and everyone. Yet, genuine silence does not relate to the external noise; it also encompasses our own thoughts or internal chatter coming to a halt. Cultivating mindful awareness means being present in the moment.

Practicing mindful awareness allows us to release built-up stress and tension in our bodies and minds. In a refuge of silence, we can release worries and anxieties through practicing mindful awareness. And I am not saying we should ignore or suppress our emotions. It is about allowing ourselves to sit with them, to see without judgment or attachment. Powerful healing and self-care are essential in this context.

While delving into the world of silence, I stumbled upon something mind-blowing. It has a profound impact on our relationships - with ourselves and with others. When we embrace the silence, we create space for the serious self-reflection and introspection. It is in these moments that we can dive deep into ourselves, ask those terrifying questions, and face our fears and insecurities head-on. We know ourselves on a whole new level. Establishing a positive relationship with ourselves promotes meaningful and authentic connections with others. Seeking peace amidst today's chaos is comparable to searching for a needle in a haystack.

And let us not forget about communication. Silence plays a massive role in nurturing healthy communication within relationships. When we learn to shut up and listen to others, we create an environment of trust and understanding. We release our own need to fill the silence with our own words. Instead, we hear and honour the experiences and perspectives of others by embracing the power of silence. It is a game-changer!

If you are pondering, alright, but is there genuine proof to help this entire quietness?

So, here is the deal - silence is not an empty air. It holds a great deal of potential. It becomes possible to tap into our inner wisdom, intuition, and creativity during those moments of silence. Creating a connection with our genuine selves and unleashing our limitless potential happens during moments of calmness.

Incorporating silence into our lives is not always a walk in the park. We live in a world that glorifies noise and constant stimulation, so it takes some serious effort to create those moments of stillness and cultivate that mindful mindset. But the rewards outweigh the challenge. When we embrace silence as a tool for self-care and stress reduction, we tap into a wellspring of peace, purpose, and connection.

I am not saying it is going to be easy, but I encourage you to be patient and gentle with yourself as you embark on your own journey of discovering the power of silence. Treat it as a lifelong practice, not a destination. Experiment with small steps to discover what works best for you. And most importantly, stay open to the transformative power of silence. In the following pages, I will share stories of individuals who have embraced silence for self-care and reaped incredible rewards. Let their stories inspire you, and may you find that peace, purpose, and connection in the silence.

Silence as a Lifelong Practice

We experience a constant bombardment of noise in our lives, including the ringing of our phones, the hustle and bustle of everyday life, and the never-ending hamster wheel of thoughts in our heads. Silence, amidst chaos and commotion, holds the power to bring about change.

Silence enables a profound connection between ourselves and the world. Inner peace becomes more than a simple fairy tale. And by making silence a regular part of our lives, we can experience growth and transformation that will transform us.

Now you might wonder, "How do I bring silence into my daily life?" Well, it starts with a commitment. Like how we prioritize time for exercise or socializing, we must also allocate time for silence. It could adjust the alarm clock to wake up earlier to enjoy some quiet time, or taking a break during lunch to find peace away from the noise. Whatever we do, we got to make silence a non-negotiable part of our routine, no ifs, and, or buts about it.

Here is a handy tip for you - create a sacred space. It could be a cozy little nook in our homes where we can retreat for the silence or a mental haven, we create within ourselves. This space should be free from distractions and set the stage for deep reflection. You could try lighting an aromatic candle, burning the incense, or playing soft tunes to create the vibe. By creating this special space, we are telling ourselves and the universe that silence is damn important, and it deserves our time and attention.

But wait, silence is not something we experience when we are sitting alone with our thoughts. We can bring it into all our everyday activities. Ever heard of mindful eating? It is all about tasting and savouring every single bite, paying attention to the textures and flavours. And how about taking silent walks in nature? Embracing the undisturbed beauty of nature's sights and sounds. We can practice silence in conversations, listening without interrupting or judging. By infusing silence into our everyday activities, we are turning them into opportunities for growth and connecting with ourselves and others on a whole new level.

With silence, we should approach it with curiosity and openness. We got to wonder about it, explore it, and figure out what works best for us. Perhaps it is meditation, deep breaths, or scribbling in a journal. And we got to be open to whatever insights and wisdom may come up during moments of silence, trusting that they are leading us towards something bigger and bolder.

And it is not only me expressing all this silence stuff. It is real. Countless ordinary people have chosen silence as their way of life, and their stories are inspiring. Take Emma, for example. She was a high-powered CEO drowning in work stress and burnout. But she made silence as her saviour. Every morning, she would rise early and embrace the stillness. And you know what happened? She tapped into her intuition, made clearer decisions, and found the peace she thought was out of reach. Not only did she succeed in her career, but she also found the fulfilment she had long sought.

There is Mark, a dad, struggling with anger issues. He incorporated moments of silence into his daily routine, whether it was taking a quiet stroll or meditating for a few minutes. Guess what? That silence helped him uncover the deeper emotions driving his anger, and he became more patient and compassionate towards his kids. He transformed his relationships and created a harmonious family life.

These stories show that silence holds greater significance than just a moment of peace. It is a lifelong practice that can rock our worlds. It is a tool we can whip out when life gets messy, helping us uncover the real us, and connect with something greater in this noisy world.

As I remember the words of Rumi, that legendary poet who said, "Silence is the language of God. All else is a poor translation." In the silence, we glimpse the divine within ourselves and others. Silence holds the answers and peace we seek. So, let us embrace silence as a lifelong practice and tap into its transformative power. Trust me, you will not look back.

CHAPTER 6

Conclusion

The Journey Continues

As you reach the end of this book, it is only natural to wonder, "What comes next? How can I continue my journey of silence and its profound effects on my life?" Well, dear reader, fret not, for I am here to offer you guidance on how to carry forward the invaluable lessons you have learned. Silence, a skill worth mastering, requires practice and persistence. It is not a onetime task you can cross off your list. Rather, a lifelong commitment to nurturing the stillness within you and allowing it to guide your actions and interactions with the world. So, let us delve into the practical ways to continue exploring and practicing silence beyond the pages of this book. Keep in mind that silence extends beyond the meditation cushion or moments of solitude, allowing it to guide your actions and interactions with the world. You can incorporate silence into every aspect of your life. Whether you engage in corporate relationships, nurture family connections, navigate various life situations and workplaces, or embark on a journey of personal growth and transformation, incorporate silence as your trusted companion. In the realm of corporate relationships, silence can be a powerful tool for effective communication and conflict resolution. Pause before reacting to a difficult situation or argument. Allow the silence to settle within you, giving you the clarity and wisdom to respond with grace and understanding. By embracing silence, you create space for dialogue and collaboration, fostering a harmonious work environment. In family relationships, silence can work wonders. We often find ourselves caught up in the chaos of daily life, overwhelmed by the constant noise and demands. But by incorporating moments of silence into our interactions with loved ones, we deepen our connection and understanding. Practice active listening, not just to the words spoken, but also to the underlying emotions and unspoken desires. Embrace the silence that blooms between conversations, in those moments that true connection flourishes. Silence can be a guiding force in navigating various life situations and workplaces. When faced with uncertainty or hard decisions, take a step back and allow silence to give you a clarity and intuition. Trust your inner voice, for the noise of external expectations and societal pressures often drowned it out. By embracing silence, you can tap into your genuine desires and make choices that align with your authentic self. As you continue your journey of personal growth and transformation, silence will be your greatest ally. Set aside dedicated time for silence and reflection, be it through meditation, journaling, or sitting in stillness. Allow yourself to unravel the layers of your being, to explore the depths of your thoughts and emotions. In the silence, you will find the answers you seek and the courage to embark on fresh paths of self-discovery. Beyond these practical applications, the exploration and practice of silence is a personal and individualized journey. There is no one-size-fits-all approach. Find what resonates with your soul and brings peace and alignment. Trust your intuition and experiment with different techniques and practices. Embrace the silence that speaks to your heart. Remember, dear reader, that this book is but a stepping stone on your path to silence. It has laid the foundation and ignited the spark within you. It is now your turn to continue the journey. Let the lessons learned here be a guiding light as you explore the infinite depths of silence, weaving it into the very fabric of your existence. The journey continues. Embrace the silence, and may it lead you to the profound and transformative depths of your being.

Final Reflections

As I sit here, pen in hand, ready to write my final reflections on the power of silence, I cannot help but feel a profound sense of gratitude and awe. It has been quite a journey, exploring the depths of silence and its impact on our lives. As I wrap up this book, I invite you, the reader, to reflect on your own journey with silence and its transformative impact on your life. Recall a time when silence had a significant impact on you. Perhaps you have experienced it, a moment of solitude where the world disappears and silence prevails. Perhaps it was during chaos and noise, when you sought solace in silence, discovering peace amidst the turmoil. For me, one of the most powerful experiences of silence came during a trip to the mountains and vast plains. I drove for hours, surrounded by the beauty and grandeur of nature. Only in a secluded spot, far from everyday noise, did I grasp the power of silence. I sat on a rock overlooking a vast valley and closed my eyes. As the sounds of birds chirping and wind rustling through the trees faded away, I experienced a profound silence that seemed to envelop me. I experienced a profound connection to something beyond myself, oneness with the universe. In the stillness, I reflected on my life and the choices I had made. I realized that silence had always been there, waiting for me to embrace it. It had provided me with the space and clarity to listen to my inner voice, guiding me towards a path of authenticity and purpose. And so, as you reflect on your own journey with silence, I invite you to consider how it has changed your life. Did it give you moments of clarity and insight? Has it helped you find peace amidst chaos? Has it allowed you to connect with something greater than yourself? In our fast-paced, noise-filled world, we often view silence as a luxury. But in those moments of stillness that we find our truest selves, our deepest wisdom, and our greatest potential. By embracing silence, we empower ourselves to navigate the complexities of life with grace and resilience. When you close this book and re-enter the noisy world, remember that silence is always accessible. This sanctuary offers moments of peace and reflection whenever needed. It is a tool that we can use to cultivate self-awareness and growth. And most importantly, it is a source of empowerment and possibility. So, my dear reader, may you always find the courage to create space for silence in your life. May you embrace the transformative power it holds and allow it to guide you on your journey towards a life of authenticity and purpose. And may your final reflection be a testament to a profound impact that silence can have on our lives.

ABOUT THE AUTHOR

Kishore Mutalikdesai is a seasoned professional with a rich background in engineering and IT. He holds degrees in Electrical & Electronics Engineering and Finance. Over the years, he has held various roles in both manufacturing and IT sectors, serving clients across the globe. In addition to his professional endeavours, he shares his expertise as a visiting faculty at a prestigious business school and is the author of two non-fiction books.

Following the success of his debut book, 'Dust Yourself Off: Know your worth, pick yourself up and soar!' Kishore has returned with his latest work, 'The Power of Silence: Finding Peace, Purpose, and Connection in a Noisy World.' In this book, he delves into the significance of silence in life, career, and relationships. Drawing from his personal experiences of finding solace in silence during travel, pranayama, and meditation, he aims to impart these insights to his readers. He believes that embracing silence can bring about peace, purpose, and deeper connections in our increasingly chaotic world.

ACKNOWLEDGEMENTS

In loving memory, I want to express my deep gratitude for the role my grandparents played in shaping who I am today. Their presence in my life was a precious gift from above, guiding me with their wisdom and unwavering support. From my earliest days, I thrived under their care, surrounded by their boundless love. It is with hindsight and maturity that I truly appreciate the profound impact they had on me. They were my first mentors, instilling in me valuable lessons and virtues. I am forever thankful for the blessings they bestowed upon me. Honoring them in this book is my humble way of expressing my eternal gratitude.

Parents hold an incredible power to shape their child's life. The person I have become today is a testament to their nurturing and guidance, which I see as a kind of enchantment in my life. I extend my heartfelt thanks to my parents through this message. I can only imagine the pride they would feel if they were here to witness my achievements and growth.

Thankful to my wife Nalini for her constant support and for keeping me sustained with her delicious food. Additionally, the love and respect of my son Mihir greatly enhanced my ability to write.

Thankful to Sweta Samota, India's leading Book Coach and India Authors Academy for the support.

Thankful to Amazon platform for publishing and sharing my books.

REFERENCES

"Stillness Speaks" by Eckhart Tolle

"Silence: The Power of Quiet in a World Full of Noise" by Thich Nhat Hanh

"Silence In the Age of Noise" by Erling Kagge

"Digital Minimalism" by Cal Newport

"Mindfulness on the Run" by Dr Chantal Hofstee

Also, by the Author, available on Amazon.

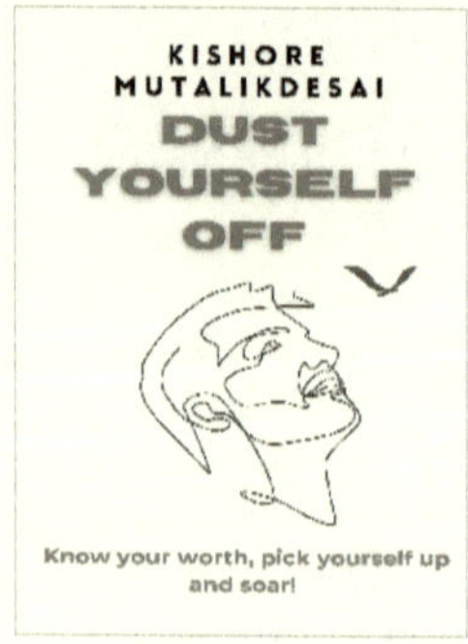

www.ingramcontent.com/pod-product-compliance
Lightning Source LLC
La Vergne TN
LVHW041732190726
843493LV00007B/2317